Bipolar Disorder Survival Guide

How to Manage Your Bipolar Symptoms, Become Stable and Get Your Life Back

Sara Elliott Price

Published in The USA by:

Success Life Publishing

125 Thomas Burke Dr.

Hillsborough, NC 27278

Copyright © 2015 by Sara Elliott Price

ISBN-10: 1511740329

Disclaimer

Every effort has been made to accurately represent this book and its potential. Results vary with every individual, and your results may or may not be different from those depicted. No promises, guarantees or warranties, whether stated or implied, have been made that you will produce any specific result from this book. Your efforts are individual and unique, and may vary from those shown. Your success depends on your efforts, background and motivation.

The material in this publication is provided for educational and informational purposes only and is not intended as medical advice. The information contained in this book should not be used to diagnose or treat any illness, metabolic disorder, disease or health problem. Always consult your physician or health care provider before beginning any nutrition or exercise program. Use of the programs, advice, and information contained in this book is at the sole choice and risk of the reader.

Table of Contents

Introduction 1

Chapter 1: What's Up, Doc? 3

Chapter 2: Causes, Triggers & Types.....................9

Chapter 3: Life in the Fast Lane.......................... 17

Chapter 4: The Depths of Despair? 24

Chapter 5: Help Yourself! 32

Chapter 6: Never Walk Alone 38

Conclusion... 45

Introduction

Chances are you're looking at this book because you've been told you have bipolar disorder.

But maybe you only *suspect* you might have it and need to be sure. You've experienced mood swings that can't be explained any other way, highs and lows that have begun to take over your life. Or maybe you wonder if someone else—your partner or child, or a friend, might have bipolar.

Whatever the details of your case, you're now considering a future made up of unpredictable ups and downs; depression and elation, where you may be unable to control your feelings and may even behave at times in a way that's completely irrational and bizarre. What's going on? How are you going to cope? And is there anything you can do about it?

Well, the short answer is yes. There are plenty of options for you to try and tricks to pick up. You can learn to identify your triggers and recognize when an episode is beginning. You can take steps to minimize your highs and lows through therapy and lifestyle changes. You can put strategies in place to be able to cope.

This book gives an overview of bipolar disorder before going on to look at what options there are to help you. We'll look at what you can do to help yourself, how you can help others to help you, and how you can learn to take control as you cope with life on the rollercoaster.

As some people reading this may be going through an episode of depression or elation when concentration is difficult, we'll sum up the key points at the end of every chapter. That way you can skip the boring bits if you want to!

Chapter 1: What's Up, Doc?

Let's start by taking a look at bipolar. When does moodiness become a problem?

Maybe you've known for a while that you have bipolar disorder. But maybe you've just found out, or only lately begun to suspect that you may have it.

Bipolar is known for its extreme mood swings with more normal periods in between. But these aren't the same for everyone. Some people have shorter periods where they feel "normal" and frequent, but less extreme, mood swings. Some are mainly depressed with just moderate highs.

Because of the differences, the condition is split in two. Bipolar 1 is the classic elation and depression (mainly elation), and bipolar 2 is hypomania and depression. Hypomania is a lower "high," so someone with bipolar 2 is mainly in a depressed state. We'll be looking more at these terms later.

Isn't it just being moody?

Bipolar is pretty much misunderstood by non-sufferers. Someone might say, "What are you making so much fuss over? So you're moody – who isn't?" Well, that's true. Many of us have bad moods or mood swings from time to time. Hormones and stress are two obvious causes for ups and downs in our moods.

Some people believe these ups and downs mean they can identify with someone with bipolar. They might say things like, "You should have seen me last week – I was so emotional when I watched that movie!"

Other people believe their emotional changes could mean that they have bipolar. But it could be that they're just moody by nature, or going through a difficult time. Not everyone who feels a bit down or unhappy now and again has clinical depression, and it's for sure not everyone who feels excited and happy needs to see a doctor!

So when does moodiness become a problem? When should you seek help for your mood swings? Well, if you've not been diagnosed but you're worried about your moods, or you think you may have bipolar, you need to see a doctor as soon as possible.

The problem of diagnosis

For some people, the fact that they have strong mood swings has brought them a diagnosis. Even though you may take weeks or months (or even years) to switch from one to the other, these moods can be pretty extreme if you're not on medication. It's very likely that your friends and family have noticed them, because your feelings of depression and elation (known sometimes as mania) are becoming kind of obvious.

On the other hand, many people are thought to be only suffering from clinical depression. No one knows that they might actually have bipolar disorder until the depression lifts and their mood ends up swinging the other way. Even then their good spirits can just be put down to the fact that they're feeling better.

It can take some time for a diagnosis, because who goes to the doctor when they feel well – better than well, in fact? So the doctor doesn't see you when you're "high" and the diagnosis is missed. He or she will diagnose you as "unipolar," that is, suffering from depression. No wonder that maybe even now you're not really sure.

Why does it matter?

Some people choose not to be proactive about their bipolar. Their attitude is "Why do I even need a diagnosis and medication? Does it matter if I get high without drugs and want to give everyone a great time? And if I'm depressed and don't want to talk to anyone, it's my problem, not theirs!"

Are they right? Well, yes and no. It may be true that no one experiences bipolar in quite the same way as you do, so it *is* a personal issue. Some people cope with the condition while being very successful in holding down a high-powered job, for example. Others struggle with suicidal thoughts and repeated hospitalizations. But if you haven't yet found a therapy that helps, having bipolar disorder isn't only *your* problem. It affects all those around you and, as you may have noticed, it can stop you living a normal life.

The highs and lows of bipolar can be devastating. And although we might feel we're coping okay, when we're not thinking straight we don't always notice that things are getting out of control. You may get pretty sick without even noticing.

Depression can lead to fatigue, poor self-esteem, feeling lost, empty or unworthy, being unable to work, problems with eating or sleeping, self-harm, substance or alcohol abuse, addiction and thoughts of suicide. Sufferers tend to withdraw from society. They have no energy, may stop taking care of themselves and become isolated, which only makes the depression worse.

Elation (the "high" or manic episodes) can make you overactive. You have loads of energy and this can make you lose your inhibitions and behave out of character. It can make you do crazy things like suddenly deciding to start a business or get married to someone you barely know, buy a house or car for someone or give away all your money because it seems like a great idea. When you come down off your "high" the idea doesn't seem so great after all.

Taking responsibility

Both depression and elation affect your judgment and your ability to concentrate. This can be especially serious if you have responsibilities. You may have young children at home who need you to be able to care for them. Or you might have projects and meetings at work where you need to make some big decisions.

Even if you don't have major responsibilities, you need to be well to cope with the basic tasks of our daily lives. Take areas like driving, dealing with everyday expenses, trying to juggle your studies or work with domestic tasks like shopping, cooking and laundry, and being aware of your personal safety in dangerous situations, from crossing a busy road to going into unsafe urban areas at night.

If your mind isn't functioning properly, either because you're depressed or because you're going through a manic episode, you can very easily put yourself and others in dangerous situations. Or you may start to overlook little details and life can quickly begin spiralling down out of control.

Does any of this sound familiar?

Having bipolar can be pretty lonely. There's still a stigma, or shame, surrounding mental illness, and most people are going to need some help. They also need the support of knowing they aren't on their own with this condition. Don't try and cope alone! There are things you can do, and taking responsibility for your illness is a great start to being back in charge of your life once more.

SUMMARY

Bipolar disorder is more than just being moody; however, you should see your doctor if you're concerned about your mood swings.

If you've just been diagnosed with bipolar, you should be aware that it can affect your judgment and ability to focus.

Help is available! You may not feel like accepting it right now, but you can learn to take back control.

Chapter 2: Causes, Triggers and Types

Let's start by taking a general look at bipolar. What do we know about it? What causes it? Can I learn what triggers an episode of depression or elation?

Bipolar affects both men and women, in about equal numbers. It usually starts when someone is in their 20s or 30s, but for some it starts as a teenager or even earlier.

The condition used to be called manic depression, or manic-depressive illness. The name refers to the highs and lows that sufferers experience in the classic bipolar mood swings. It's only in the last few decades that the name has been changed to bipolar disorder, and there is more general understanding of the condition.

Early texts show that way back in ancient times a number of doctors and writers in different countries knew about a condition of temporary insanity that took the form of mania and sadness. They recognized it was different from other forms of mental illness or madness.

Over the centuries studies revealed more understanding of bipolar as we know it today. However, experts couldn't agree about the cause. Some claimed it was due to a biological cause; that is, something in your genes. Others said it was down to some psychological or psychosocial reason – a life experience that affects your mind.

So what *does* cause bipolar disorder?

The jury's still out on this one. Experts still don't have all the answers, but we know more than those early medics did. At least we can put the clues together and come up with some probable answers, although basically it seems there's no single cause for the disorder.

Family. Firstly, bipolar seems to run in families to a certain extent. This suggests that there is a genetic link. In other words, there's some physical problem which can lead to bipolar, or make us more likely to be affected by it. But some people are the first in their family to have bipolar, so this can't be the only reason.

Neurons. Secondly, we now know that bipolar can be treated with certain types of medication, notably anticonvulsants and lithium, which is a mood stabiliser. These drugs affect the brain and central nervous system, so we can deduce that bipolar is a disorder of the electrical and chemical circuits in the brain.

So what does this mean? Putting the two together, it seems that some people may be more likely to get this nervous disorder because they have a close family member with it, but in any case it seems to be triggered by some external factor or event.

It's very important to remember that although it's to do with the mind it's not imaginary! As the website bipolar.about.com puts it, "While we're at it, let's be clear about something: a mental illness is one that *affects* the mind, not one that's all *in* the mind."

Triggers for bipolar

Stress. It seems that something we go through can be a trigger for bipolar in some cases. One of the most likely suspects seems to be a very stressful experience. Many people can look back and pinpoint an upsetting or traumatic event, such as bereavement or divorce, which seems to have been the start of it all.

A lot of the research into bipolar seems to show stress can be a trigger. This could be a stressful home or work environment, physical illness or social issues. Stress on its own may not be a direct cause of bipolar, but together with other problems it is surely a strong suspect. Anyone with bipolar has to take care to avoid getting stressed.

Disturbed sleep. Experts now believe that lack of sleep can be a trigger for bipolar. This could be because the brain is unable to find healing and freedom from stress if we can't sleep. Getting a regular eight hours and monitoring your sleep patterns can help you avoid a bipolar episode.

Childhood trauma. Another possible link is a stressful childhood. In some cases a child who has experienced emotional trauma – maybe abuse and neglect, say, or intense grief and loss – can get bipolar as their young brain develops and tries to deal with on going stress.

Reaction. Psychiatrists believe that for some people bipolar may be a reaction to serious issues in their lives. For example, someone who's depressed may find escape through a manic episode. The supreme overconfidence may conceal someone who's really lacking in self-esteem.

Medication. Certain kinds of over-the-counter or even prescribed medication may be a trigger for a manic episode for some people. Antidepressants are known to do this, so they aren't usually prescribed for bipolar depression. Other drugs include some brands of cold medicines, corticosteroids, appetite suppressants and even caffeine.

Substance abuse. Hitting the bottle or using street drugs can trigger an episode. It can also make bipolar worse in the longer term. Depression can be triggered by alcohol and tranquilizers; cocaine, ecstasy and amphetamines can all be triggers for a manic episode. If you're using alcohol or street drugs to help you cope with bipolar, you're making things worse for yourself! Get help now.

Seasons. Some people find their bipolar episodes follow the seasons of the year. Depression is more likely during winter, spring and fall, while mania is more common in the summer.

Other kinds of bipolar

Did you know that not all bipolar is the classic case of highs followed by a period of "normality" then depression some time later? Here are a few variations that someone with bipolar may experience, either as a one-off or several times.

Rapid cycling

For some people the depression can go on for months or even years, but for others the cycles come round more quickly. This can change from time to time, so anyone with bipolar might sometimes experience this faster changeover from one state to another, with maybe just a couple of weeks between them.

Rapid cycling bipolar can be more difficult to manage. However, medication such as lithium is a great help in most cases. If you haven't already got a diagnosis, you should definitely see your doctor and get the medication you need.

Sadly, people with rapid cycling bipolar that aren't very well controlled are more likely to end up hospitalized, as in some cases the risk of attempted suicide is very high. There is also a higher risk of substance abuse.

Mixed bipolar disorder

Some people with bipolar experience mixed episodes, where the mania and depressive episodes come along at the same time, or switch rapidly from one to the other. It's thought this might be more common in people who develop bipolar at a younger age, but anyone could experience episodes like this.

Although it seems to be impossible to have two such opposites at the same time, no one said a mental illness had to be logical! You might be showing signs of a high, or manic, episode, like laughing and talking rapidly, then collapse in tears. Or you could appear depressed and upset but say you've never felt happier. Then, even a few minutes later, the emotions might switch the other way. Mixed episodes can continue for days or even weeks.

This kind of bipolar is more difficult to control, but regular, ongoing medication helps. The drugs used are likely to be mood stabilizers and antipsychotics. ECT therapy has also been helpful when medication doesn't work.

Cyclothymia

There is another disorder closely related to bipolar: cyclothymia. This is a very much milder form. Often the person with this disorder may not even notice the mood swings, and many people who do know they have it refuse medication. That's because the fairly moderate highs of hypomania are enough to fire them up to be creative and innovative. They can focus on projects without worrying about the extreme symptoms of full-blown bipolar.

But in some cases the depressive episodes are enough for them to seek help. Once the symptoms of either elation or depression get worse, the person is considered to no longer have cyclothymia but bipolar.

In the next couple of chapters we're going to take a closer look at mania, hypomania and depression. What signs should we be looking out for?

SUMMARY

Causes: Bipolar is a disorder of the brain neurons. There is a genetic link in some cases, with bipolar running in families.

Triggers: There is a range of possible triggers that can lead to someone developing bipolar or having an episode. Stress is the main suspect.

Types: Other kinds of bipolar, which you may experience, include rapid cycling, mixed episodes and cyclothymia.

Chapter 3: Life in the Fast Lane

As we've already seen, a person with bipolar usually has periods of emotional highs and lows, with a more normal period between the two. In this chapter we're going to take a look at the "highs" of bipolar. These are called mania and hypomania.

The term "mania" may be upsetting as it brings to mind someone in a movie who's running dangerously out of control – a maniac. But according to the Merriam-Webster dictionary, it can mean:

1. Mental illness in which a person becomes very emotional or excited

2. Extreme enthusiasm for something that is usually shared by many people

So the medical term came first; it's just been high jacked in popular opinion to mean something more.

For some people these highs can be extreme; for others it's not so obvious. The episode could even be missed by friends who don't know you well. So what happens during these highs? What should you watch out for? And are they always a bad thing?

The second pole

To start with, no one can be diagnosed as having bipolar unless they've experienced a high. These highs are called episodes of elation, euphoria or simply mania.

Why do we need a high to be diagnosed with bipolar? Well, without a high the doctors will put you down as "unipolar," that is, suffering only from depression. Bipolar means two poles; unipolar means one pole (as in North and South Poles – at opposite extremes). If they don't know about the highs, maybe for the very good reason that you haven't experienced one yet, they can't give you that extra "pole." And without the extra pole you can't get the right treatment for bipolar.

Have you ever watched those pole-vaulters at the Olympics? They use a long, flexible pole to help them reach amazing heights, soaring high in the air feet first in a way that would be impossible on their own. That's what our second pole does for us. Okay, we don't get a medal, but we sure do fly.

The symptoms of mania

Having a high might feel good. You've probably noticed everything seems to speed up. You talk fast, you feel wired up, you make plans and embark on new ventures. You only need a couple of hours' sleep a night and just grab a bite to eat on the run, because you can't sit still for long. It's great, right?

Well, let's take a closer look at one of these episodes of mania. According to the website bipolar.about.com, you might experience any or all of these symptoms. It might just be one.

As you can see, there's no way you could imagine these things during a period of depression! Some sound great. On the other hand, others may be taking things a little further than you'd normally be comfortable with.

No time to sleep. You need very little sleep and don't even feel tired.

Energetic. You're full of get up and go; it's like an adrenaline rush. You're restless, talking fast and your thoughts are racing away.

Over-confidence. Suddenly you feel that nothing is beyond you. It doesn't matter if whatever you're thinking of is actually dangerous or even illegal.

Poor concentration. You find it hard to focus on one thing at a time because your mind is rushing on to the next thing.

Poor judgment. Because of your higher self-confidence and inability to focus you're more likely to make wrong or dangerous decisions.

Short tempered. You may be irritable and aggressive with those around you, especially if they don't seem to be moving at the same pace as you or don't agree with what you're doing.

Flashy behaviors. You abandon your usual habits and reflect your new confidence with flamboyant clothes, reckless behavior and extravagant spending. You may also abuse drugs or alcohol.

Lack of inhibition. As well as outspoken speech and inappropriate behavior, you may have a greater sexual appetite and practice some risky sex activities.

Delusions. A symptom of a manic episode can be delusions, for example that you alone are right and everyone else is wrong. A sense of your own importance is a common delusion. This can lead to domineering and irrational behavior.

Hallucinations. You may see or hear things that other people can't.

These last two points show a break with reality – you can no longer distinguish between the real world and what you imagine. Psychologists call this *psychosis*. This only happens with the most severe episodes, but it can happen. This type of mania is known as *mania with psychotic symptoms*.

Don't worry – not everyone will experience all these symptoms with every manic episode. But the list is enough to show that a high period is not all about soaring through the air. Apart from the behavioral problems, sooner or later you have to come down again. That can be very traumatic in itself and even plunge you straight into depression.

While you're having a manic episode you might not be really aware of your unusual behavior. It's only afterwards that you realize what you've been up to. This might actually come as quite a shock, especially when you see the effects on those around you. You might also have some unpleasant consequences to face.

So does everyone with bipolar go through this as an alternative to depression? You might wonder if it's worth it. At the very least, you stand a chance of making a fool of yourself, alienating your friends and losing all your money!

Well, some people only experience very moderate highs. This is called hypomania, and we'll be taking a look at that in a moment. There is also treatment in the form of medication that can stabilize the moods, and being aware of your triggers can help avoid an episode too.

Later in the book we'll be looking at practical steps you can take to predict when a manic episode is coming, and how you can limit the effects of your reckless behavior during a manic episode. If you can't wait, see Chapter 5.

Hypomania – the lower high

Some people don't go through this kind of manic phase. Their high episodes are less obvious and might be missed altogether. Let's take a look at the kind of things someone with hypomania might experience during a high.

Energy. They feel great, able to get on with life and brush off snags and difficulties, which would have been paralyzing while they were depressed.

Creativity and focus. Their strength is centered on projects and problems. They have the energy to come up with great ideas without going over the top.

Confidence. They have complete confidence in themselves while still able to take on board what others are saying.

Someone with hypomania may still show some unusual behaviors. They may be reckless or inappropriate, but they don't suffer hallucinations or delusions in the same way that someone going through a manic episode may do.

If you experience hypomania, you may be diagnosed as having Bipolar 2, which means periods of depression followed by milder manic episodes.

SUMMARY

The manic part of bipolar is important because it enables a diagnosis, otherwise you would just be diagnosed as having depression.

During a high the person will show a range of energetic, reckless and unusual behaviors, which may include hallucinations and delusions.

A milder form of mania is called *hypomania*.

Chapter 4: The Depths of Despair?

As we all know, the other extreme of bipolar disorder is depression. In fact, you could say it's literally the polar opposite of the manic episodes we've just been looking at.

You probably know all about depression, right? But not everyone experiences it in the same way; some people suffer more badly than others. One person may just feel glum and low, while another will be at breaking point.

It seems that now we don't use the old name, manic depression, non-sufferers can forget that the main part of being bipolar is going through long periods of depression. But the same chemical and electrical problems in the brain that can trigger the better-known manic episodes are also responsible for the depressive episodes.

So let's take a closer look at depression. When we talk about a depressive episode what does it mean? Well, to start with we'd better cover what it *doesn't* mean.

Sadness. People use the term "depressed" when they're feeling a bit low. "I'm really depressed – I just split with my boyfriend/girlfriend," they might say. Sometimes they might say this over pretty trivial things. Maybe someone they secretly like is getting engaged to someone else, for example. Or maybe they've put on an extra pound. At other times the problem might be a bit more serious, like failing to get a job they applied for. These things are frustrating and can happen to all of us, but we don't normally feel down for long.

Situational depression. At other times we might react to the stress of a major life event and become depressed. This could be due to something like losing a loved one, or getting divorced. This kind of emotion is more serious, and some people manage to cope better than others. If the symptoms go on for some time and you find that you can't carry on with your normal life, it might be a good idea to get some treatment, at least in the short term. Situational depression can slip into general depression if it goes on.

So what are the signs and symptoms of depression?

If your symptoms go on for more than a couple of weeks, a doctor might diagnose major depression. Anyone with bipolar is familiar with this kind of depressive episode. The website bipolar.about.com groups the symptoms of depression under five main headings.

1 Changes in activities and energy levels

2 Physical changes

3 Emotional changes

4 Difficult moods

5 *Changes in cognitive skills (thinking and reasoning, for example)*

Let's look at these symptoms in more detail. Keeping roughly the same order as the above groups, you might experience some or all of the following.

Fatigue. You have no energy; you feel listless and like everything's too much effort.

No longer enjoying activities. You stop doing the things you normally enjoy, or you do them but don't get any pleasure from them anymore.

Sleeping problems. You may be unable to sleep, or on the other hand you might sleep most of the day.

Aches and pains. You might find you have unusual pains in your muscles and joints, headaches and so on.

Agitation or sluggishness. You may be restless, or on the other hand you may become lethargic with slow or confused speech.

Eating problems. You might not feel like eating so that you become underweight. Alternatively you might start piling on the pounds through eating too much, or eating junk food.

Sadness, emptiness and despair. We're all familiar with these classic symptoms of depression. You may cry a lot or sit and stare into space.

Poor self-esteem. You lose confidence in yourself and your abilities so you end up with a poor self-image, especially if you're putting on weight.

Feelings of guilt or self-loathing. You can start to feel bad about yourself. Knowing your loved ones are concerned can make you feel bad too. This can easily lead to substance abuse, including too much alcohol, or self-harming practices and suicidal thoughts. **If you're feeling like this, please get help straight away.**

Irritability. You may be short tempered with friends, family and coworkers.

Anxiety. You can get pretty worried when you're depressed – about the depression, your feelings and how you're going to cope, as well as other issues not directly connected with your emotional state.

Indifference. Depression can make you just not care about anything, even major events or activities you normally enjoy.

Self-criticism. You might keep on criticizing your own behavior and blaming yourself for things that are really nothing to do with you.

Poor concentration. You can't focus on anything for long, or make decisions. This can be a big problem at work.

Memory problems. It can be harder to recall things that you know pretty well, or remember tasks or items on a list.

Becoming disorganized. Last but surely not least, this can actually be one of the first signs that you're entering a period of depression. Sometimes we just can't be bothered to sort things out and our daily habits start to slip.

Delusions and hallucinations

Just as we saw in the mania episodes, someone with severe depression may experience breaks with reality. Maybe you believe bad things are about to happen. You may see or hear things that other people don't; for example, you might hear voices telling you that you're responsible for something terrible. **If you're having these kinds of symptoms you should call a doctor immediately.** This type of episode is called *depression with psychotic symptoms* and is very distressing.

Diagnosing a depressive episode

Apart from the last point, you might feel most of the above symptoms are pretty standard issue when it comes to depression, right? But when it comes to diagnosing you with bipolar, your doctor will be looking for precise symptoms in order to classify this as true depression. For example, if you're depressed because you've lost your job that's distressing, but on its own it's not a sign that you may be having a depressive episode.

American doctors are bound by the Diagnostic and Statistical Manual of Mental Disorders. This gives the symptoms that are usually seen in a depressive bipolar episode and other depressive conditions. It has various rules that apply to those symptoms too.

As well as three or four of the symptoms we mentioned above, the patient must show either a depressed mood (sad, empty, tearful and so on) or a lack of interest in daily activities every day for at least two weeks.

There must also be no other possible explanation for the depression. If you were using drugs that could make you depressive, the doctor wouldn't identify it as a bipolar episode. Or if you'd experienced a major life event like losing a loved one, which could make anyone depressed, that could be classed as situational depression.

This official manual,the Diagnostic and Statistical Manual of Mental Disorders, doesn't make a distinction between the depression experienced by someone with bipolar and general clinical depression. The accepted view is that we can't tell them apart. However, some doctors feel there may be a difference. Research is ongoing on this.

So is there anything we can do when we're suffering from depression? Yes, there is. In the next chapter we're going to take a look at ways you can help yourself through the assorted highs and lows of bipolar, but in the meantime it may help to think of it as some bipolar sufferers do: It's the weather in your mind, and in time it will change.

SUMMARY

A depressive episode in bipolar is classed as one that affects either your mood or your energy/activity levels every day for at least two weeks.

Other signs include physical symptoms like changes in appetite and/or sleep patterns, and problems focusing, remembering and making decisions.

If you're experiencing suicidal thoughts or hallucinations, including hearing voices, please seek help immediately!

Chapter 5: Help Yourself!

So far we've looked at the causes and triggers of bipolar, then the two "poles" of elation and depression. What now – is there anything you can do to help yourself? How can you learn to cope? Are there strategies for dealing with bipolar?

Well, there are quite a few. In this chapter we'll be taking a look at life with bipolar and seeking ways to make things easier. There are some excellent suggestions on the internet; the following are taken from helpguide.org.

Be proactive. To make a difference and learn how to cope with your mood swings, you need to play an active role and take responsibility for your illness.

Get involved in your treatment. Become an expert, research the disorder and all the options and work with your doctor on finding the medication and other therapies that are right for you. Then take the medication faithfully, whether or not you feel like it.

Monitor your mood. Keep a mood diary or a daily journal and note how you're feeling. Write down how many hours of sleep you had, your weight, medication and any other relevant details. This will help you watch out for early-warning signs that a change may be on the way. If you notice it early you can take steps to avoid it becoming a full-blown manic or depressive episode.

Know the signs. These are some common red flags to watch out for, taken from the *BHI Clinicians Guidebook: Bipolar Spectrum Disorders,* cited on helpguide.org. Maybe you can add your own warning signs to this list.

Warning signs for depression: You stop cooking proper meals; you become disorganized; you want to be on your own; you don't care about anyone else; you start having headaches; you become indecisive; you start needing more sleep.

Warning signs for mania: You can't concentrate; you find yourself talking quickly; you're hungry; you're irritable; you don't need so much sleep; you can't keep still.

Develop coping strategies. Build a collection of strategies to help you maintain stability when you notice the warning signs that a change may be coming. These vary from person to person, but the following may be helpful. Some strategies are covered in more detail later in the chapter.

Get eight hours' sleep every night
Talk to someone supportive and/or go to a support group
Do something that helps you relax, maybe something fun or creative

Cut back on your other activities and take time for yourself

Get some exercise

Increase your exposure to light

Get more/less stimulation

Reduce your alcohol, sugar and caffeine intake

Talk to your therapist or doctor

Tell your family and friends how you're feeling

Note your symptoms and emotions in your journal

Put an emergency action plan in place. This can help you relax, knowing that if a full-blown manic or depressive episode comes along other people will know how to help. Write down your current medication, any other health problems you have, emergency phone numbers, and who you want to look after you if you can't care for yourself for a while. You should also include what symptoms would make it obvious that you need someone else to take responsibility for you. Make sure your family or close friends know where to find this list.

Build a support network. Make sure your family and friends know about your condition and keep them involved. Choose one or two people who are steady, reliable and good listeners, and share how you feel. If any so-called friends make you feel worse about yourself, dump them!

Get out and about. Join a support group and try to build new friendships, or call up old friends. Make an effort to get out and do things, even just going for a walk. You could also consider volunteering and helping someone else who's struggling with bipolar.

Stick to a daily routine. Create stability and structure by developing a strict routine, and make sure to follow it. Set yourself times for eating, sleeping, working, exercising, socializing and so on. Make sure you get into a regular sleep pattern; avoid caffeine from lunchtime onwards and any stimulating activities in the evening, and don't nap during the day. Try to follow this routine even through episodes of depression and mania.

Exercise every day. Exercise reduces stress and improves the mood. It's now believed that regular exercise of, say, 30 minutes a day may reduce your bipolar symptoms. Walking is an easy and cheap way to exercise; you could walk with a friend, either human or canine, and have some undemanding company.

Deal with stress. Learn relaxation techniques, get a massage, and listen to the kind of music that lifts or calms you. Find out what appeals to your senses: flowers, birdsong, going to a concert or talking a walk in the country. Make your leisure time a priority and include some fun things.

Watch what you eat and drink. Choose a healthy diet with plenty of fruits, vegetables and wholegrain. Make sure you include Omega-3, which is thought to reduce mood swings in people with bipolar.

Beware of caffeine, chocolate and processed or high-carb foods that can affect your mood. Avoid alcohol and street drugs, which can trigger a manic or depressive episode. Even certain medication can have an adverse effect, like antidepressants, which can trigger mania. Make sure you talk to your doctor about any side effects, but don't stop taking medication except if you have an extreme reaction.

Hide your credit cards. Some people with bipolar lock up their cards, or leave them with a trusted friend when they feel a manic episode may be coming on. They want to be sure that they're can't blow all their cash while they're acting out of character.

Make a to-do list before you go to bed. Some people recommend this to give you a reason to get up in the morning. It helps give your day some structure and purpose when you're struggling with depression. Even if you're not going to work, you can write down things like buy milk, empty the garbage or walk/run to the park.

SUMMARY

Coping strategies can help you deal with bipolar by keeping you healthy, relaxed and aware of early changes in your moods.

Regular exercise and relaxation techniques are both great for managing stress, one of the key triggers of bipolar episodes.

Having a support network and emergency action plan are practical steps to take against serious episodes where you need more help.

Chapter 6: Never Walk Alone

In the last chapter we looked at some practical ideas for ways to monitor your health so you can be aware of early-warning signs. Then we talked about the strategies you can put in place to help you maintain a stable mood, especially once you feel that a change may be coming.

Those suggestions could be described as self-help, or drawing on your own resources to deal with the disorder. In this chapter we're going to take a look at how you can find help from others. Various therapies, friends and family, and support groups can all play a part in coping successfully with bipolar.

Treatment and therapies

As we've already seen, there are treatment options available for people with bipolar. Some people with the condition are able to hold down a high-powered or challenging job with their symptoms well controlled by medication. However, others may continue to struggle with either depressive or manic episodes, or both.

Medication is the most effective treatment for most people. You'll probably be prescribed a mixture of mood stabilizers and anticonvulsants. Anticonvulsants are drugs used to control epileptic seizures which have also proved very useful in patients with bipolar. It's believed their calming effect on the brain helps to control mood swings. If you have a severe, psychotic episode of depression or mania you'll probably be offered antipsychotic drugs, which are also very helpful.

Lithium is one of the most effective and widely used mood stabilizers. However, it's not suitable for everyone and can have nasty side effects. One of the key things to remember about lithium is to be sure to have regular blood tests to check your dosage is right, as too much can be toxic.

Be proactive by working with medical staff to create the best treatment plan, and then take the treatment that's been prescribed for you. Become a bipolar expert and talk to your doctor about any side effects of your medication and possible interaction problems with other drugs.

It's now believed that the most effective treatment plans also include various other therapies and self-help strategies, like those we looked at in the last chapter; living a healthy lifestyle, including eight hours of sleep a night, a balanced diet and plenty of exercise.

Therapy can be a very successful part of your treatment plan. It's thought that medication is more effective when you get therapy at the same time. It gives you a chance to talk about your bipolar with someone who understands and can give you support. You'll also be taught tools and strategies to use to measure your progress, keep you stable, and deal with the fallout from your depression or mania and its effect on those around you. Here are a couple of different therapies to consider.

Cognitive behavioral therapy is about understanding how your thoughts affect your emotions. You'll learn how more positive thought patterns can make a difference to managing your symptoms and how you can avoid certain triggers, like stress, through problem solving.

Interpersonal and social rhythm therapies teach you how to build relationships with those around you. If we work through issues relating to those around us we can get rid of a lot of the stress we carry about. And social rhythm therapy looks at getting stability in your life through steady routines for daily activities like eating, sleeping and exercising.

There are plenty of other complementary therapies that can also be very useful. Talk to your doctor or therapist, or check out options on a site like helpguide.org.

Friends and family

It helps to talk to friends and family. Okay, let's be honest, not everyone is very supportive when it comes to mental illness of any kind, especially anything involving depression. No doubt you've heard some unhelpful comments, like "It's all in your mind! Snap out of it!"

Trouble is, like physical pain, unless you experience mental issues personally it's hard to understand how the other person is feeling. But many people do want to help; they just don't know where to start. They might try to cheer you up with jokes or treats, for example.

Your close family, especially parents and partners, can be impacted by your bipolar too – almost as much as you are, sometimes, through stress and worry. Not being able to help can make it worse for them, so make them part of your treatment plan, and be upfront about what you're going through. Keeping things to yourself isn't really the smartest way of helping people understand.

As we've seen, putting an emergency action plan in place is an important way of helping others to help you. You can also teach them to recognize when you may be getting depressed by giving them a list of early-warning signs to look out for. Tell them what they can expect and how they can help you.

Marcia Purse, Bipolar Disorder Expert on bipolar.about.com, suggests the kind of signs that someone else might notice when you're heading for an episode of depression. These include seeing the mail or bills piling up, domestic tasks left undone (laundry, garbage etc.) and noticing when you start turning down invitations, canceling social engagements and staring at TV shows you don't normally watch.

Support groups

There's plenty of help for people with bipolar, especially online. Many useful sites contain practical advice and suggestions, with forums where bipolar sufferers can share with others who know just what they're going through.

Some of these sites offer support for particular issues or groups: parents and families of bipolar sufferers; bipolar kids; weight gain or loss through bipolar episodes; religious support groups; bipolar at work; bipolar with other physical or mental issues. Take a look at the website psychcentral.com and check out resources for bipolar to see a good list of groups, or do your own research.

You may also be able to join a group that meets near you, and this gives you a new network of friends you can call or meet up with who know how you feel. You may not always feel like you want or need anyone, but in fact having a support network is vital. And don't forget, support is mutual and in turn you'll be able to support others.

Share your story

You may like to consider using your experience with bipolar to help others and raise awareness. Maybe you could think about volunteering to help other people who are struggling – maybe kids, or those who've only just been diagnosed. Or start a blog to share your story and give support to others you've never met. Doing something like this is a great way to make other people aware of the problems faced by those with bipolar, as well as giving you a purpose.

It may not always be easy to do, but the more open and honest people are about mental illness the easier it is for others to understand. Overcoming prejudice by being upfront is a great way to help others with bipolar too.

One of the reasons why bipolar disorder has become more widely known in the last two decades was a very public breakdown by the British actor, author and presenter Stephen Fry in 1995. Stephen was appearing in a play in the West End of London, but after the first couple of days he failed to turn up for the next show. Instead he hit the road, crossed the Channel to Europe and just drove. The play folded, no one knew where he was and the police were expecting to find a body. Eventually he was discovered in Belgium.

The disappearance had been widely reported in the media, and Stephen has since been very open about his condition. He even made an award-winning BBC documentary called *The Secret Life of the Manic Depressive*. Despite continuing to struggle with severe depression, his openness has helped other people come to terms with bipolar. By raising public awareness he has also helped take away some of the shame, or stigma, that is linked to mental illness.

SUMMARY

Work with doctors to develop a treatment plan and stick to it. Include therapy and self-help strategies for maximum effect.

Talk with your family and friends so they can look out for changes and learn how to help you.

Find a good support group, either online or locally. You could even consider sharing your story with others, helping them and raising awareness.

Conclusion

Bipolar disorder can be a devastating condition. But there is help at hand. You are not alone. And although you may be a sufferer – you may even think of yourself as a victim – you can make a difference to your condition.

Everyone pictures the extreme mood swings, manic highs and suicidal lows; but what about the periods of normality in between? People who don't have bipolar tend to forget about the "normal" times. And it has to be said that for some of us these times are anything but normal. But these periods of relative stability are vital. Before we start worrying about the next mood swing, these steadier periods are an opportunity to make some changes. Now is the time to learn to create stability in our minds and in our daily routines.

Medication has already made great progress in the struggle against bipolar. But now we know that drugs are only the beginning. Maybe you haven't already had therapy; maybe you have, but you could do with more. Now is the time to go for it!

Then there are all those self-help suggestions: a healthy lifestyle, regular sleep patterns, a balanced diet and all the others. These are vital partners to the medication and therapy.

Now is the time to establish that new lifestyle and that stable routine. Put those strategies in place and stick to them. Get some exercise. Monitor your health. Talk to your family and friends. Share your story with others.

You can make a difference.

Printed in Great Britain
by Amazon